LOVE
AUNTIE
BEV
XMAS 2014

Yvette Moore
GALLERY • FINE ART INC.

MOOSE JAW, SASKATCHEWAN, CANADA
www.yvettemoore.com
(306) 693-7600

HEARTLAND

A PRAIRIE SAMPLER

JO BANNATYNE-CUGNET · Art by YVETTE MOORE

TUNDRA BOOKS

Published in Canada by Tundra Books,
481 University Avenue, Toronto, Ontario M5G 2E9

Published in the United States by Tundra Books of Northern New York,
P.O. Box 1030, Plattsburgh, New York 12901

Library of Congress Control Number: 2002101723

National Library of Canada Cataloguing in Publication Data

Bannatyne-Cugnet, Jo
    Heartland: a Prairie sampler

ISBN 0-88776-567-X

    1. Prairie Provinces–Juvenile literature.   I. Moore, Yvette
I. Title.

FC3237.B35 2002   j971.2   C2002-900773-9
F1060.B35 2002

We acknowledge the support of the Canada Council for the Arts and the Ontario Arts Council for our publishing program.

We acknowledge the financial support of the Government of Canada through the Book Publishing Industry Development Program for our publishing activities.

Printed in Hong Kong, China

1 2 3 4 5 6   07 06 05 04 03 02

A PRAIRIE SAMPLER

Years ago on the Prairies, young people were instructed in homemaking arts. Mastering the needle and thread was a required skill for pioneers who had to sew and repair their own clothing, bedding, and harness. Often they would make a "sampler" using "bits of this and that," scraps of used fabric, and sometimes bleached flour sacks to show off all the different stitches and details they could create with a needle and thread.

Early settlers made sampler quilts with a random selection of block patterns held together with a common theme such as stars or flowers. Today, many families display with pride these treasured pieces made by their pioneer ancestors.

To me, the Prairies are much like a sampler – mile after mile of repeated patterns of land and color embroidered with details of life and history – forming the fabric of this unique place I'm proud to call home.

THE LAND

We joke on the Prairies that if your dog runs away from home, you can stand in your front window and watch him for three days. Where I live, I can stand in our back farmyard and see the grain elevators of our nearest town ten miles away.

But when you travel across the Prairies, you will also see low rolling hills, steep valleys called coulees, eroded badlands, sand hills, lakes, and sloughs – all carved out by glaciers of the last Ice Age. Sometimes you come across gigantic rocks and boulders. They originally came from the Canadian Shield and were dropped off by a receding glacier. The prairie has many surprises.

The first French explorers had never seen anything like it. They called the vast treeless plain "prairie" or meadow, for lack of a better word, and wrote that it was "a sea of grass as far as the eye could see." When I stand on the open prairie under the enormous blue sky, surrounded by grass waving in the wind, I too lack the words to describe this place I call home.

The Prairies are the heartland, right in the center of North America, covering over two million square miles and stretching over three thousand miles from northern Alberta to central Texas. The Rocky Mountains to the west dictate our climate. They create a "rain shadow." When the humid westerly winds sweep in from the Pacific Ocean, they lose most of their moisture on the mountain slopes. As a result we receive less than 20 inches (500 mm) of precipitation (rain and snow) per year. This, over thousands of years, has left the Prairies dry and able to sustain only grasses.

Fire has also played an important role in creating the grasslands. Often started by lightning, prairie fires were swept across the land by wind. Everything in their path burned. But fire only burns the top of the grass, leaving the roots, many extending 12 feet (3 m) underground, unharmed and ready to start growing again the next spring.

Trees, on the other hand, never stood a chance unless they were close to a long-term water supply like a river or lake. There are more trees on the Prairies now than ever before. They have been hand-planted and watered to provide shelterbelts to homes, habitats for wildlife, and to keep the land from blowing away. Any prairie fires are quickly put out. In fact, they say we have so many trees now that the early settlers wouldn't recognize the place – but we still don't have a lot of trees.

THE CLIMATE

Our weather patterns include hot summers that see temperatures over 100°F (38°C) and cold winters that drop to -50°F (-46°C). We experience definite seasons – spring, summer, fall, and winter. For variety add rain, snow, hail, and dust – all brought to you courtesy of our constant wind. And they say "if you don't like the weather, just wait ten minutes and it will change." In fact, we hold the world record for temperature change recorded in a single day. It happened in Montana. It went from 44°F (7°C) to -56°F(-49°C). *Burrr!* That's a change of over 100°F (38°C)!

We also have the distinction of one area of the Prairies being referred to as "Tornado Alley" because of the number of twisters that pass through – up to 150 per year. I am not referring to the annoying dust storms or dust devils, where we watch our land blow away and we can only pray for rain. Tornados have wind speeds that can range from 99 to 298 miles per hour (160 to 480 km/h) and cause horrendous damage – destroying buildings, tossing cattle into the air, and even carrying away locomotive engines. Fortunately because our population is sparse and spread out, we usually escape harm. But on hot, humid days we are watchful and ready to head for the safety of the basement.

Hot days also produce hail – small pieces of ice that fall like rain. Hail can be devastating because it can wipe out our crops in addition to causing property damage. Hail usually ranges from pea size to golf ball size. The Canadian record hailstone fell about 25 miles (40 km) from our farm. It weighed 2/3 of a pound (290 gm). The United States' record hailstone fell in Kansas and it weighed a whopping 1 pound 11 ounces (503 g). Did I mention snowstorms and blizzards? Did you know these can happen any month on the Prairies? Cattle can be seen huddled in a July snowstorm! When it happens in the summer, it's a novelty and the snow melts quickly. You have to work fast if you want to get a snowman built. Blizzards are extreme snowstorms lasting from four hours to forty-eight hours. In winter these can be very dangerous because of freezing temperatures and low visibility from blowing snow. One can easily become lost. Many a pioneer froze to death making his way back from chores. Stories are told of settlers tying a rope around their waist before leaving the barn so they didn't lose their way, and sometimes this wasn't enough. Nowadays the best advice is to just stay home. Kids like these days the best because schools are closed as a safety precaution.

We respect the weather, we take precautions, and we're all in it together. Enduring these weather extremes gives us bragging rights. Everyone on the Prairies has more than one weather story. The one thing we truly like to brag about is that we have more hours of sunshine throughout the year than anywhere else in North America – and we love it! Also, at the end of each day, we are usually rewarded with spectacular sunsets that leave us with a sense of awe for our world.

No doubt about it – prairie people are weather people. We watch it. We savor the changing seasons, and we accept that weather runs our lives.

THE PEOPLE

In a pasture close to our farm, there are circles of lichen-crusted rocks embedded in the prairie. They are called tipi rings. These circle clusters can be found all across the Prairies and are a reminder of the people who lived here before us. The rocks were used to secure the poles and buffalo hides of the tipis – a portable housing used by the nomadic tribes of the Plains Indians. Some former encampments have only a few tipi rings left behind, but there have been sites found with over 250 tipi and fire circles. I've seen 100-foot (30 m) diameter medicine wheels, the rocks arranged with up to 28 spokes. At the hub is a cairn of rocks. They are a mystery. No one knows what medicine wheels were used for, but we recognize them today as sacred sites.

The Natives lived in harmony with the prairie cycles – the migration of the bison, the cycle of the seasons, and the cycle of life. They believed in the power of the circle – the sun, the moon. Even their homes, boats, pottery, and baskets were round, all made from what the land provided.

With the arrival of Europeans, this delicate balance was upset. Europeans brought with them horses, gunpowder, and the power of square thinking – they lived in square houses, inside square trading posts, and sent out surveyors who divided up the Prairies into squares for ownership. The Prairies were surveyed into mile-by-mile squares called sections. These sections were divided into quarter sections. Each quarter contained 160 square acres. This was all very bewildering and foreign for Natives.

At first there was a mutual exchange of knowledge and survival skills. A trade relationship developed and there were advantages to both parties. The Natives' travel had been limited to walking and using dogs to haul goods. Horses made life much easier, particularly when hunting the bison, which was central to their survival.

The bison, often called "buffalo," provided for all their needs – food, clothing, and shelter. Later, in the early 1800s, these same magnificent herds were a huge attraction to the newcomers, who wanted their meat and hides and often killed them just for sport. This was very troubling to the Natives and led to the beginning of territorial disputes. In short order, the European settlers, equipped with rifles, brought the bison close to extinction. From herds of millions, they were reduced to only 500 in the late 1800s. The Natives' way of life was destroyed and they were left with no alternative but to accept the ways of the newcomers. Vulnerable, their chiefs made treaties with the governments of the day and soon they were confined to life on reserves (in Canada) and reservations (in the United States).

The demise of the great bison herds made it easier for European settlement. The huge beasts, weighing up to 2,000 pounds (907 kg), roamed freely and trampled everything in their path. Governments of the day were quick to launch huge advertising campaigns encouraging settlers to come West to farm. Promoters with posters were sent throughout Europe. They promised land, prosperity, and freedom – "Homes for Millions. The Best Wheat Land and the Richest Grazing Country under the Sun." The people came. They first trickled in on horseback, then they came by ox carts and wagon trains carrying everything they owned. But it was the completion of the railroad that broke the dam, and settlers poured across the prairie. Hundreds of thousands – from the British Isles, from the Scandinavian countries, from France, Holland, Poland, Russia, Italy, Switzerland, and the Ukraine.

Each settled on their quarter section square. One hundred and sixty acres of land was more wealth than many could have ever dreamed. To prove their claim, settlers were required to clear and plough the land, plant and harvest a crop, and build a house, all within three years. To register their claim cost ten dollars. It sounded easy enough.

But it wasn't. Many a newcomer was totally unprepared for this new land.

At first they would search out anything familiar – often they chose poorer land simply because there was something there – a cluster of rock, a coulee, sloughs – anything – instead of a field of grass, which would have been be easier to farm. Even to be close to someone from the same country could have been part of their decision about land. And, of course, the new immigrants came from all walks of life, from many countries with different religious backgrounds, language, and customs. Many just were not farmers.

There was much adaptation and adjustment. Imagine using bison dung for fuel and the great outdoors for your bathroom. Some could afford building materials for a house; others had to make do with what their homestead provided. Some were fortunate to have trees; others had only the prairie sod. Many used a combination of the two. These soddy homes were easy to build and fireproof. They were warm in winter, and reasonably solid. But they were impossible to keep clean and if it rained for several days outside, it could rain inside for a week. A good roof often became the deciding factor on whether newcomers stuck it out or not. Others could not cope with the extreme weather, which the posters and recruiters had failed to mention.

Often, the isolation, loneliness, drought, and infestations of grasshoppers made it difficult for farmers to raise the money necessary to register their claim, even if they fulfilled all the other requirements. Four out of ten homesteaders failed to "prove" their claim. If they had money, many returned to the Old Country. Others fled to the closest town.

The first prairie towns tended to start up by a water source – a lake or river or even a spring. Later towns sprung up along the rail lines, approximately 10 miles (16 km) apart. These usually started with a railroad station and a water tower for the steam locomotives, then a general store and post office, followed by a land office, bank, and a hotel. Sometimes these were housed under one roof. As prairie commerce grew, more stores and service industries like blacksmiths, lumberyards, and grain buyers moved in. These were followed by churches, schools, and newspapers to meet the needs of the many families. It was during these very hard beginnings that the Prairies took on the name "Next Year Country." The new inhabitants were always hoping for a better crop next year, a better price for their crops – next year, and they were always working towards a better life for their families – next year. One can only admire the determination of these pioneers to stick it out and work together to make the Prairies their home.

AGRICULTURE

The Prairies were once flooded by an ancient sea, then covered by an ancient forest, and finally scraped smooth by glaciers of the Ice Age. Grass became established. And so nature prepared the soil for agriculture. The bison were a part of this prairie ecosystem. But once the bison were almost eliminated, ranchers were quick to take advantage of the plentiful supply of grass. Huge herds of cattle crossed the prairie under the watchful eye of the hired hands – cowboys. The beef industry still supplies the large city markets of the East.

Next came the settlers wanting to "prove" their land. It was only natural that these new farmers would plant grass. The fields of tall grass on the east side of the Prairies were planted to corn; the shorter grass more to the west was ploughed under and seeded to wheat. Both corn and wheat are cereal grasses and are well suited to the prairie growing season – they say you need 100 frost-free days to grow a crop. Corn and wheat remain major crops, but many new crops have been added for diversification and survival of the prairie farm. We grow wheat, durum, oats, lentils, flax, canola, mustard, and chickpeas. Other farmers grow potatoes, soybeans, canary seed, hemp, barley, sugar beets, rye, sunflowers, beans, and field peas.

The first farms were a quarter section in size – 160 acres. Farms are much larger now. There are farms that are a full township in size – that's over 23,000 acres. When the first farmers – sodbusters – tried to plough the land, they struggled to break through thick, root-bound sod. It was with the invention of the "chilled steel" plough, by John Deere, that they began to make progress. They say that a farmer and an eight-team hitch of horses working 8 hours a day for 20 to 30 days could seed 300 acres. The Prairies came to life with innovative-thinking farmers looking for better ways to work this new land.

The tractor arrived on the scene in the 1920s. By the late 1940s, the technology of this harnessed "horsepower" of a fuel engine allowed farmers to work 24 hours a day if they wished, at speeds four to five times faster (and no horses to bed and feed at the end of a hard day). Harvesting a crop had been done by hand, using a large curved sickle. Threshing crews – many men and horses – replaced the sickle. The combine has replaced two to three threshing crews. You can harvest 150 to 200 acres per day.

Farms of the past all had livestock. Everyone had horses, a milk cow, and a few chickens. A large garden was a necessity. Mixed farming gave way to specialization in either crops or livestock. And the livestock has changed. You're just as likely to see emus, ostrich, elk, or bison as cows, chickens, sheep, or hogs.

The pioneers hauled 100-pound (1 2/3 bushels) bags of grain by horse-drawn wagons or flat beds to the nearest train depot, which might have been over 50 miles (80 km) away. Then big wooden grain elevators, an American invention, sprang up all across the Prairies. These were the very first prairie skyscrapers – the tallest buildings for miles around. Branch lines of the railroad went off in every direction, with an elevator as their delivery point, reducing the travel to 10 miles (16 km) or less for most farmers. And because that's where farmers went to do their business, small communities grew up around these delivery points.

Next came the invention of the one-ton grain truck in the late 1920s. Thus began the love affair with the truck, which continues to this day. Every farmer wanted one. Often it took years to be able to afford one. Trucks of all sizes provided transportation over debatable roads in all kinds of weather conditions.

Our reasons for using them have not changed. Grain elevators are being torn down and railway branch lines are being ripped up. Small communities are disappearing. Huge cement terminals are appearing as the most efficient way to handle and transport the grain for the grain companies and railroads. Farmers once again are forced to haul their crops long distances and must adapt by hauling larger loads with even bigger trucks – big semis and super "B" trains holding 800 to 1500 bushels. There're more trucks per capita on the Prairies than any place else on earth.

The biggest change in farming is the cost. At one time land was a dollar an acre. Now the price ranges from $250 to over a $1,000 per acre. Tractors cost more than a house. Combines are up over $300,000. The cost of other machinery, fertilizer, and bins all continues to rise. What has not changed from the pioneer days is that many a farmer goes to bed wondering if he or she can cover expenses.

We get pictures taken of our farms – from the air. It started when barnstormers would fly across the Prairies. Their aerial photographs were a novelty, and selling the photos helped them pay for their gas. Farmers like to have aerial photos taken every few years so they can see their work-in-progress – the old homestead. Many homes have a special display on their wall of these photos.

MINING

Deep below the surface of the Prairies lie coal, potash, oil, and gas. The discovery of these natural fossil fuels and by-products from our prehistoric past are a boon to our economy. Thousands of people work in the recovery and processing of mineral deposits.

Early explorers discovered the coal seams that became the most common source of heat for the pioneers. We use cleaner burning fuels, such as natural gas, for our homes. Coal obtained by strip mining using giant shovels is still the least expensive method for producing steam to run the turbines at our power plants.

Potash or potassium carbonate was accidentally discovered when companies were searching for oil approximately 2/3 of a mile (1 km) below ground. The world's largest potash mine is located in Saskatchewan, near Esterhazy. Potash is used in fertilizers and is exported to the world's farmers.

Oil or petroleum is known as "black gold." Landowners are usually delighted with the discovery of oil under their property. It means that farmers will receive financial compensation from an oil company using a drilling location on their land, and yearly rental if oil is found and a permanent well site established. If farmers happen to have the mineral rights, they will receive a percentage of the profits.

Wells were actually punched into the ground by dropping a sharp bit over and over again – for weeks on end. Hard to imagine they made much progress. Now they use a rotary drill, which is much faster and can go deeper. The average vertical well is 1,640 yards (1,500 m) deep. In a field close to where we live, they drill horizontal wells. They start out going straight down, then turn and go sideways. I always wonder how they know where they are. Years ago drilling for oil was a rough and dangerous job. Experience in the oil patch was the best teacher. Today our universities and technical schools have special degree programs to prepare future geologists and engineers for work in the petroleum industry. Even though we have degrees and computers out at the sites, it's still hard work and a dangerous job for the "roughnecks." Many a farmer has worked in the mining industry to get his or her start in farming. Many a farmer still works to supplement declining farm income when crops or markets are poor.

WILDLIFE

As a child growing up, I had plenty of time to explore the Prairies with my friends. We spent hours investigating holes. The Prairies are full of holes. Holes dug by animals. There are tiny holes dug by ants and spiders, and much bigger holes dug by badgers. Mice, swallows, owls, prairie dogs (gophers), rabbits, and garter snakes live in in-between size holes. We would poke sticks down these holes to see how deep they went. Sometimes we'd fill in the holes with the surrounding excavated dirt. We'd check daily to see if the hole had been reopened by the tenant, and usually it was. Never did an animal poke its head out when we were there. We would have died of fright if it had. We are lucky that animals on the prairie avoid humans and have no interest in us as food.

The open prairies do not offer many places to hide. Animals here survive by speed or camouflage – blending in with their surroundings. Many also burrow and hide in the sod and have a series of underground "condominiums" for different purposes – sleeping, storage, birthing, and so forth. Coulees and sloughs provide most of the habitat for animals today because much of the Prairies is now cultivated for farming.

Before European settlement in the 1800s, wildlife was plentiful. Many species have become extinct or are endangered because we have not been good stewards. Our numbers of each animal have been drastically reduced.

We're always fascinated when we discover evidence of the past – a flint arrowhead or tiny fossilized seashell gives us as much pleasure as a scientist who uncovers the fossilized bones of a Tyrannosaurus Rex. We often read in newspapers of yet another dinosaur dig revealing more about this ancient chapter of prairie history. It's hard to believe that over 200 million years ago, these dry old prairies were once a lush forest jungle and that dinosaurs ruled.

In our farmyard, I have had deer looking in my front window at me. Muskrats try to take up residence in our dugout. I have caught raccoons breaking into our granaries, trying to snack on our grain. Boy, did they look surprised! I've seen antelope leap over our pasture fence. Did you know that they can cover up to 27 feet (8 m) in one leap? They're the fastest animal in North America and have been recorded running 70 miles per hour (113 km/h). We have thousands of birds – ducks, geese, hawks, cranes, and many others use our fields for a "bed and breakfast" as they make their migrations north and south. My favorite bird is the western meadowlark. It is identical to the eastern meadowlark. The only way to tell them apart is by their song. The western meadowlark sings a flutelike melody of six to ten notes. It is unique and beautiful. No matter how I am feeling, whenever I hear it sing I always feel better.

It's a toss-up for which is the cutest animal on the Prairies – burrowing owls or prairie dogs. Burrowing owls are very tiny. They live in holes in the ground dug by other animals. They are becoming extremely rare and efforts are being made to increase their numbers. Prairie dogs or gophers are also quite small, but certainly more plentiful. Both owls and gophers are fun to watch. Porcupines, rabbits, badgers, prairie chickens, pheasants, and partridges are all in the neighborhood. At night, when I am out looking at the stars or the Northern Lights, coyotes howling across the valley often serenade me. It makes me feel a part of the Prairies.

PLAY

Every spring, sloughs are replenished with runoff, melted snow. By fall, these shallow bodies of water are dried up. But in the meantime, sloughs are critical habitats for many animals and insects. There is a lot to observe and to investigate. Who can resist a chance to go rafting? Be careful – if you slip into the water, you'll be up to your knees in muck.

Hay season transforms fields of grass and alfalfa into bales of all shapes and sizes. We put up hay bales to feed our livestock through the winter months, when their grazing grass is under snow. The large round bales can weigh up to 1,500 pounds (680 kg). They can be moved only by a tractor. Bales are good for hide-and-seek. Our barn cats use these bales to hide their new kittens. For children the bales are like playground equipment.

Winter is our "down" time from work. It's natural that the most popular sports would be played in winter and on ice.

Curling is a sport in which two teams of four slide stones across the ice towards a target. The object is to have the team's stone be the closest to the "bull's eye" – the center of the circle target. Each team has a skip, a third, a second, and a lead player. The skip holds a broom over the target area to provide direction for the stone thrower. To assist in the stone's delivery (speed and accuracy), teammates sweep the ice with brooms, clearing the way.

Scottish settlers brought curling to the Prairies. It was a sport for both men and women. It caught on quickly and curling rinks popped up in just about every town. It was often too cold to play outside. In 1909, the world's largest rink of the day was built in Regina, Saskatchewan. Folks in Saskatchewan have fond memories of Sandra Schmirler's rink winning three world championships and topping it off with the first Olympic gold medal in 1998.

Jam can curling was the young peoples' way of being like the grown-ups. They played on a homemade outside rink or dugout. A neighbor remembers, when he was growing up, that laundry and bath water were thrown onto the streets, and he curled on the slimy smelly ice that was created. Empty jam cans were filled with sand and water and left outside to freeze. An old spoon was sometimes placed in the middle, with its bowl part sticking out. This served as a handle. When young people played the game, there was no target other than the skip's broom. Many a dispute arose over whose jam can was closest.

Hockey is so popular on the Prairies that people continue to play in the form of road hockey, using any grid road or town street – just as long as it is smooth. Many young boys dream of one day playing in the NHL and many boys' dreams have come true. Prairie folk are proud of our "crop of boys" who made it to the NHL – Gordie Howe, Mark Messier, Theoren Fleury, Bryan Trottier, and many others. One amazing family, the Sutters, who lived on a farm near Viking, Alberta, had six sons all play in the NHL. Now that's a bumper crop!

FOOD

The people who call the Prairies home come from many different countries and cultures. This is never more apparent than at a community potluck supper, where everybody brings a specialty to share. The incredible variety of food might include perogies, lasagna, Swedish meatballs, curried chicken, beef stroganoff, and Chinese fried rice. These delicious foods are a good example of what we gain by acceptance of each other's traditions and customs.

There are some foods that are distinctly "prairie" such as saskatoons and bannock and, some would say, jello salads!

Saskatoon comes from the Cree word "mis-sask-quah-too-mina," which means "berries." This prairie fruit, also called Juneberries, was a major food source for the Natives and the early explorers. Bison (buffalo) meat was dried, pounded into a powder, and mixed with saskatoons, wild rice, and buffalo fat to make pemmican. Stored in buffalo hide bags, it would keep indefinitely. This was the first "packaged convenience food" on the Prairies – easy to carry and to cook – just add hot water!

These days, saskatoons are most popular in pies or with ice cream. Perhaps you'd like to try these favorite prairie recipes.

SASKATOON PIE

Pastry for a two-crust pie
4 cups (1000 ml) saskatoon berries
  (sorted and washed and drained)
¼ cup (50 ml) sifted flour
½ cup (125 ml) sugar
1 teaspoon (5 ml) salt
¼ cup (50 ml) butter or margarine
2 tablespoons (30 ml) lemon juice

Line a medium-sized pie plate with pastry. Fill with washed, drained berries. Mix sugar, flour, and salt and sprinkle over berries. Dot with butter, sprinkle with lemon juice, and cover with top crust. Perforate the crust with a fork and carefully seal the edges so that the juice will not overflow in the oven. Bake 45 minutes at 400°F (200°C).

Bannock, a biscuit made from flour and water, was introduced by the fur traders to the Native population. With the arrival of the pioneers and wheat as a primary crop, flour became readily available and a natural staple. Bannock can be cooked over a campfire, in an oven, or on a stovetop.

CAMPFIRE BANNOCK

4 cups (1000 ml) flour
8 teaspoons (40 ml) baking powder
3 cups (750 ml) cold water (approximately)
1 teaspoon (5 ml) salt
1 tablespoon (15 ml) sugar

Mix dry ingredients. Make a hole in the center. Add water to make a thick batter. Pour into a greased fry pan. Place over campfire. Turn when bottom part is brown. Cook until both sides browned. It's delicious served with butter and chokecherry jelly.

ARTS AND CRAFTS

Prairie people used what was on hand to express their creative bent. Folk arts had both a practical purpose and were pleasing to the eye. Some crafts, like wheat weaving and *pysanka* (decorated eggs) came with the people who immigrated to the Prairies; others, like birch-bark biting, were homegrown.

Birch-bark biting is a traditional Cree art form. Bark that is unblemished is harvested and peeled into paper-thin pieces. This is the hardest part. When you have a large enough piece to work with, you gently fold it two or more times like you would to make a paper snowflake. By biting gently into the bark with the eyetooth, an image is made. You bite, then rotate the bark, bite, and rotate.

Originally the birch-bark biting was used as patterns for quill and beadwork on clothing. I have seen pictures of bugs, birds, flowers, and geometric shapes. I am always amazed at the closeness and consistency of these tiny bite marks. I marvel at how anyone can do this when they cannot see what they are doing. The Native people who do this art form say it teaches patience. This art form was almost lost but is now – I'm glad to say – experiencing a revival.

Working with grass or wheat is an ancient craft and was practiced in many countries. The names of patterns reflect their origin – the Welsh Fan, the Arabic Cage, the Swedish House Blessing. With over sixty varieties of grasses on the Prairies, it's natural that the craft would be done here. Wheat weaving is popular today and has reached new levels of creativity and craftsmanship. I recommend that the beginner start out with something simple.

DIRECTIONS FOR THE STAR OF DAVID

To work with wheat, you must first harvest or purchase wheat stems with the heads intact. Trim off the excess, just above the first node on the stem. Peel off the outer casing. Soak the wheat for 20 minutes or more. Roll it in a towel for 30 minutes, so it is pliable.

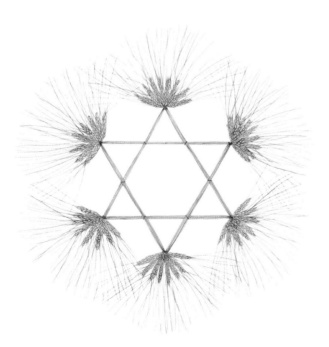

MATERIALS FOR THE STAR OF DAVID

48 straws with head 10 inches long
Waxed dental floss

1. Divide the 10-inch straws into 6 groups of 8.
2. Tie each bundle below the heads. (A clove hitch knot works best.)
3. Tie 2 groups together using heads of one bundle and butt ends of the second bundle.
4. Continue tying in same fashion, adding 1 more bundle to the first 2. You should now have a triangle shape, with wheat heads on each point.
5. Repeat steps 3 and 4.
6. Place 1 triangle on top of the other, making the Star of David. Tie to secure in place where straws cross each other.
7. Other decoration may be added as you choose.

The Ukrainians who immigrated to the Prairies brought the craft of *pysanka* with them. *Pysanky* are raw eggs that are decorated as ornaments and meant to be kept indefinitely. Eggs were a cheap and a relatively available canvas for the elaborate decorating skills of the Ukrainian women. For many, making pysanky helped ease homesickness. It was a way of holding on to their heritage and it was a part of the Christian Easter ritual. The egg is a symbol of new beginnings. To give these beautiful eggs to someone is a way of wishing them well.

In the beginning, the women used traditional designs, but in time their new home influenced new designs. Color choices were still important as each color had symbolic significance. Yellow represented a successful harvest and wisdom; green represented innocence and youth; blue meant good health, and so on.

Using a *kistka*, which is a pen that writes with melted wax, a design is applied. The egg is then dipped in yellow dye. More design is added after the dye dries. The egg is dipped in a darker color, and after it dries, more wax is applied. This is repeated until the last color, which is black. The final step in the process is to melt and wipe off the wax.

TRADITIONS AND CELEBRATIONS

On the Prairies, we have so many different traditions to celebrate: powwows and square dancing jamborees, wheat festivals and jazz festivals, fowl suppers and fundraisers, fairs and rodeos. Every town puts itself out for at least one big celebration each year.

Someone once made the comment about "sleepy little towns on the Prairies." They're right – everyone's tired from going to so many events, and most people volunteer to make sure these events happen. Young and old volunteer. It's a prairie tradition.

We think about our past and prepare for the New Year at the Christmas season. School is out and holidays are legislated. It's a time when families and friends gather, often traveling many miles through winter conditions. It's a time of good food and goodwill. It's a time we thank our lucky stars we live on the Prairies, and wish on a falling star that others could have what we have.

People who live on the Prairies are like
the timeless grass. Just as the grass has deep
intertwined roots, so do we as a people. They
say "If you grow up on the Prairies, you may
leave the Prairies but it will never leave you."